73

Amulet
a collection of poetry

ᜁ

by Jason Bayani

Write Bloody Publishing
America's Independent Press

Austin, TX

WRITEBLOODY.COM

Bayani, Jason.
1ª edition.
ISBN: 978-1938912-18-4

Interior Layout by Lea C. Deschenes
Cover Designed by Anthony Wyborny
Author Photo by Steve Young
Proofread by Helen Novielli
Edited by Meg Hurtado Bloom
Type set in Bergamo from www.theleagueofmoveabletype.com

Printed in Tennessee, USA

Write Bloody Publishing
Austin, TX
Support Independent Presses
writebloody.com

To contact the author, send an email to writebloody@gmail.com

MADE IN THE USA

AMULET

I will break God's seamless skull,
And I will break His kissless mouth,
O I'll break out of His faultless shell
And fall me upon Eve's gold mouth.

— Jose Garcia Villa

AMULET

1

2

3

B-Sides

1

Remaking the Line

The line recasts itself, pulls in toward the skin unbuckling
the knot in my ribs, an aperture shuttering the empty sweep
again and again and again. The word falls out of focus.

STRANGE VELOCITY

Surviving America is learning
the limit of want. Holding
your ability to name. I live
in the noiseless rooms
of your discomfort. Easy
to be written over. Whose free
we fighting for?

PLAYGROUNDS AND OTHER THINGS

Finally, let me say that I think my poem… is not "racist" but "racially complex." —Tony Hoagland

I'm a runaway slave-owner. —Iggy Azalea

I.

Eighteen, and every day
the city expands inside my lungs. I live in full,
heaving breaths, like I finally made it to a clearing
where the white kids couldn't catch me.
And we boys, bold and buried in swagger
slapped on with so much bad cologne.
That day in the city,
bass piping out of our spindly forearms,
we erupted into downtown
like we could dap the streets for all their shine.

And the old lady leaning into the wind
at the corner of Sutter and Stockton:
I heard her tell it like broken glass,
"Go back to your country."

Couldn't get angry enough to breathe right;
tried to remember if there was a word for what makes you
suddenly clutch your chest.

II.

Now imagine being told that she was only
trying to understand her racism (it's complex, you know).
Art is what happens to her. You need to let it hang in the air.
There is Art to recognition, the Art is in the naming,
Art is a mirror, you can make Art out of this.

There is no Art in being safe. You must risk uncomfortable truth.
The experience is not yours alone. This experience
is not owned by you. We've heard this story already.
This is Art. Art rejects the familiar. Stop telling this story
already. The story is the old woman in her sunglasses
marveling that three brown boys would presume to be so
comfortable.

III.

Imagine being asked to applaud
and feeling guilty that it takes so long to remember
you have hands.

Racism is not interesting. It is not an intellectual pursuit.
It is the guts.
One word is a trigger. One word can break your posture. We break
knuckles on this.
Watch where you put it.

IV.

I'm willing to say that we share
this particular sandbox equally.
You just have to let me kick sand in your face
for thirty years or so.

V.

I, too, find it real easy to talk about
how much I hate white people. It's a pastime.
I eat that shit with my morning cereal.

What is more difficult
is the velocity of how I love you. There, dawg,
is all the complex racism any one of us can handle.

Depression

I.

A lot of people say that writing is their therapy.
Me, I go to therapy.
I never really wanted to write poetry, I just like coffee.
That's a lie.

I want to scream some days.
But then I gotta ask myself,
Does this scream really capture
what I'm feeling right now? Does it have
the right sonic qualities? Is this how
I want people to remember my frustration?

I'm a perfectionist
when I'm motivated. And today
I might only be motivated to make cookies.
Really good fuckin' cookies.

I'm tired of smart-ass motherfuckers
making some crack about how I'm a writer
when I'm quiet and I don't have much to say.
I got shit to say. I just don't know what that is yet.
Too many people don't want to think before
they make noises.
I can do that too. Buy me a drink.

II.

I do like people. Sometimes I like you so much.
I love the things you say, so much.
And I sit here, muttering under my breath, "I'm about to cut
that fucking mouth right out of your face,
you wonderful motherfucker.
That's my mouth. You have my mouth.
Why can't I say shit like that?"

III.

Imagine we're in a room, and everything in this room
has a mouth except for me. I feel that most days.

My mouth wants misanthropy. It wants to spell
"misanthropy" in front of little Asian spelling bee champions
and tell them to step back because I'm still the future of Asian America.

Most of the time I feel I am without my mouth. Like my mouth
has been seeing other people. My mouth
has been using other tongues.
My mouth has been screaming on someone else's picket line.

My mouth just can't get over this shit already. My mouth
left the house today without me. My mouth left because
I watch it all from the wrong side of the window.
My mouth always got one foot out the door. My mouth
looks back at me, heart clenched,
telling me if only I spent as much time making use of my mouth
as I do coming up with metaphors for where my mouth is...
And the only song I know is, "Baby, please,
baby, please."

IV.

I am a poem. But I don't want to be a poem every day. There's too
much person here. Person sings sometimes too. Badly in the shower.
Person sings off tune. But we sang before we talked, didn't we?
Before the first person

could call a thing a thing; before we could share exactness, be able to
say, This thing in my hand means the same thing to you as it does to
me. Before all of this, there was song, a switch in tones that spelled
"hurt" or "happy", the shape of the melody so we could know there
is a thing that feels and wants to be heard. And that the mouth waits,

and waits.

Skin

To be dark in your own culture is a quiet study
in the art of disarmament, to remember
your palms, the color of your palms, show them
your palms. They are not the rest of your skin.
Nobody wants to be reminded
that skin is a luxury. My palms are surrender,
flat and giving, a body tumbling into rubric;
palms whiter than slaughterhouse milk.

I give my palms (this is not an appeasement)
a burrow into all of your safe spaces. Place
is temporal—the first lesson you learn when
you are taught how not to be comfortable
in your own skin. I was just trying to walk by,
I never wanted to be such an interruption.

PULLING THREADS

Everything in my head is the sound, word
without shape. I'm waiting for this to become a thing,
or for it to make me interesting. I practice
getting my handshake right so I don't have to say anything.
I'm not dreaming this. Poems are what happens
when you close your eyes. Stars are fathomable.

Last night I dreamt I was writing poems about waking up.
The night is coffee. The stars are home. The woman you love
is dancing alone in the bedroom.

I'm looking for a place where I can fill some space. I fill
lots of space. Lots of pretty fuckin' space.

Yesterday she asked what must "happy" look like for me? I gave her
the answer I thought should go on my epitaph. This is why, she tells
me, I can only speak in front of a microphone.

I'm not afraid of you.
I'm just afraid you'll make me
see me, and one of us will have to walk away.
Part of me feels I deserve a cookie for saying that.

A man's ability to feel is overvalued in Art.
I've cashed in on it.
Every woman who loved me
hates me a little for that.

I owe something more than poems. Maybe a really good
chili recipe, or a second word for thunder. Or maybe
more sentences that include the word "you." I dig you.
You make me happy. You can be a real dick
sometimes. Watch how I love you, asshole.

GRISTLE

I don't know what to do with myself most of the time.
It's like I'm twelve again at the school dance,
and I've been practicing the running man all week.
And I'm standing there,
and I keep telling myself, "This ain't the right song yet."
And I know that I can do the running man,
My running man is hella fresh. And it's never
the right song yet. Even when they're playing Rob Base,
it ain't the right song yet. And by the end of the night
everyone is slow dancing to Keith Sweat
and I'm doing the running man in front of the bathroom mirror.

A few years back I went on a ten-day silent meditation retreat.
On the second day it snowed and I woke up
to a steady stream of people rolling their luggage down the hill.
On the fifth day I cried into my instant coffee
because I had nowhere else to go.
On the eighth day I built a snowman. Two hours later it melted
and fell on its back. An hour after that someone else built
another snowman facing it, with a branch sticking out of its groin.
Then, when I went to the meditation hall,
halfway through the session,
everyone around me started farting.
I know that sometimes with me
it's all heading to the dick and fart joke,
but I work hard at this, you know?
Trying to find sanctity, a beatitude.
I'm still looking for God, okay? But farting is funny to me,
and I wanted to laugh so hard my heart hurt.

HELLA

Vengeful heaven, where is your wrath? —Francisco Balagtas

I. Cain

This life upon the hem of your garment—
I ask, how do you make a home of rootless
pasture? My brother's blood, I can still smell
blood in the profitless soil. My father,
forgive me. I lost us Eden again.
There is no home for me here anymore,
you marked the path East upon my marrow,
and the land has offered no place to dig.

Know now, it was not fist or stone that killed
my brother. The weapon resides within.
It is a red immense. It lives between
the spaces of our fists. Others will find it.
As you have marked me, I have marked you too.
This is how the long war begins: in a clutch.

II. Sonnet for the "War on..."

This is how the long war begins. In a clutch
of thunder. The rustling river. A body
up-ended. Armistice at the end; there's no
way around it. All things fold back in-

to dust sometimes. The weapon resides within
a contagion until all falls out of form.
All that we are: personified armaments,
an elocution upon the lower registers,

a shout that would tear down a city's walls.
This is the covenant. This is the script.
The all-consonance a staccato hunger.

The drawing advance. A numbered finality.
An end fumbling toward a completion.
A deviation at the start of all things.

III. The Source Wall (after Jack Kirby)

A deviation at the start of all things.
Clockwork in variance. How do you determine
the metrics of the unmovable? The aged futility,

language, an artifact in deliberation.
The divination of restrained thought, a mangling
wire. The tightrope is blunt metaphor. What if

life is a matter of escaping the equation? To higher
planes where they read our failure in four-color
panels. Tranquility is an apathetic audience.

The wall of thought is a wide canvas. Someone
keeps painting the void as a ubiquitous mural.

What if the solution ends up with indivisible
numbers? What is left, other than
contemplating the music within a shape?

IV. Sonnet for Jessica

Contemplating the music within a shape,
rooms without tone; something of a jazz cliché,
the thick emptiness behind locked and bared teeth.
There, the cold zephyr soft-shoeing across
your skin. Adagio for a closing fist. Why
must I put the picture together? A rasping
floorboard the only living document of your
great leap across. Tell me I'm not my mind.

Tell me the low harmonics are only that,
a dull racket, and the sky a soft seizure.
I've been thinking of you dying alone,
head tilted, your slow smile with a labored bent,
palms opening like white flags. A last
call. This, the red immense. An abandoning.

V. Sonnet for a Bar Fight

Call this the red immense. An abandoning
fault line. The space levied between our fists;
rushing madness as a killing tool; Biblical
murder weapon which scripture gives no name.

All of you jawed petulant. Holding a mountain
heart like a muzzled tide. Look at what you
made me do. Irises opening like
rusted switchblades, bodies built into bombast.

There are days still where you cannot shake it,
can't get loose from the weapon, and prayer
is an intercession upon curled fists.

Can't shake the frenzy, arms set loose, flailing
wild into the ether, the ruddy nowhere,
the halo-point of any burning city.

VI. 1-7-09

The halo-point of any burning city
is where gunpowder and prayers converge.
The hallowed lament of mothers who've watched
helpless before the gardens inside their sons' chests
split the world into unmanageable pieces.
Tears are what catalyze the rust grooming
the flaking skin of singed archways. There's no
sure hand when fury itches itself to kindling

and feet stomp the sidewalk cracks that break
our mothers' backs. The street a scorched vein
pockmarked by people holding each other: discarded
lovers. The slow fracture of a city block,
a metronome quaking inside their rumblers' wrists,
a dream fevered, that lusts to shape the world.

VII. Spree

A dream fevered, that lusts to shape the world
back into refinement. This is my patriot
mind, not one with a trigger finger like mine.
What is the God formula? How do you break
the firmament? A bullet escapes the barrel
at 400 meters per second. Call this
the world breaker, a splitting of tongues.
Tell them they'll come for you like they have for me.

Where is my country inside all of this?
There's nothing left but the long collapse—
the life broken down to the tick of a slow clock.
My hate, it is elegant. A weightless certainty
that speaks a hell that holds no diction until
there are language purists whose ears do sever.

VIII. Sonnet for E-40

There are language purists whose ears do sever
at the cleaver's tongue buried in the mouths
of colored men. A phrase, though, must be turned.
How else does one see God in this language,
when it's the mirror that never looks back?
There are words that deserve to be murdered
by apostrophes. Words that must be slacked
by slumped tongues. Consonants ripped from their cased
housing. The audacity to increase
your baller status to ballatician.
Not enough to feel, you got to smell me.
A language yearns to spurn governance,
it begs to be impeded upon,
broken neck slung from an 808 bass drum.

IX. Sonnet for DJ Q-Bert

Broken neck slung from an 808 bass drum,
the thump is internal. It starts with a thump,
the wet grazed thump that sparks synapse and mars
the stoicism of body to wide agape.

The thump is the beat, the beat is a wild zephyr;
that must be why the creation of Art
feels like caging the wind. And why you feel
music is defined as moveable objects.

To pull the slap off wave crest tops—submit
the rolling form to memory. The hand
begins to shape discord to composite arcs,
a cauterized scar harmony pressed down

on spinning vinyl; atop the turntable
the beat reshapes, the heart is pliable.

X. Sonnet for Lauren

The beat reshapes. The heart is pliable,
a slow slung to face, a labor toward breath.
I want you to see me in composition,

the respiration of me, the long build back to
an artisan garden, a fracture framework,
me in the world as implemented piecemeal.

I been trying to juke the narrative,
trying to dust off a flat surface. A place
between the indentations. A safe place for spines.

Maybe all this living comes down to the encryption—
today I'm working with simpler mathematics:
"Jason+Lauren." I wrote that shit on a tree.

Give me the petal that hits like a heavy brick;
my sky, I watch it fall in measures.

XI. Sonnet for Daniel Johnston

My sky, I watch it fall in measure—
the devil that's in the downpour. A restless
etching. The canvas, yes, it is the devil;
the devil, yes, it lives in Texas. Yes,
the devil is in the numbers. What is the God
formula? The life equation, it was meant to be
this way. Some of us were meant to fall, yes, fall.
To be like a ghost: it is more than the purity
of spirit, a washing-over of past sins,
a devil rebuked. It is a simple clarity,
the devil is in the obscurity. Yes.
Life as a matter of in-between,
a return to blank page and empty space.

XII. After Manny Pacquiao

A return to blank page and empty space:
this was how I was born, in opposition. The hard
sell living on the give and take of my mother's
left hand. The sweeping hook of the barrio
in my father's right. We were born to outrun
"nothing." So we'd never have to say it like
they did, "We came from nothing." But nothing
never did nothing but keep coming for us.

Here is my education in living: to slip
the margin for an open shot, to turn
so deep into your left cross it pulls apart
the skin to pulp at the base of your foot,
the trench physics of the stick-and-move,
until the world falls into a hard focus.

XIII. Sonnet While Listening to Blue Scholars

Until the world falls into a hard focus,
a thread back to origin and organism—
the protract liturgy, the source locus.

When beginning is the word and the word is a revision,
we still build forward from a broken system.

This is me, making a living in the free-fall back.
The hardly living. The shred at the garment's hem.
The low tide at a fifth of Gentleman Jack.

Give me an anthem for the rooted gut,
the hollows of our palms, the wellspring ruckus.

I'm open. The swick of my pen is the murder cut.
A requisite magic, a search for a place for us.

This is the back-breaker's work—grab a shovel.
We make abstract fabric from stockpile rubble.

XIV. Sonnet for Mesej and Jaylee

We make abstract fabric from stockpile rubble,
mayhem at the margins; a gutted theadbareness
born brilliant against the bordered rut.
No one in the bahay got swagger like us.

Call this a mirth in the mudwork, slapbox
revival. Rotgut symmetry. The raw
mechanics of prime numbers. A wrecking
wheel spinning motherfucker it's spinning.

We are groundwork transitioning to flying
haloes. The uncertain tether of a B-boy's
hallowed back. We are built like that. We are
built like that. The rock strata. The sweetest cut.

The weapon reborn. The American stain.
As they marked us, so we have marked them too.

XV.   Dark Matter

Broken neck, slung from an 808 bass drum,
my sky; I watch it fall.   In all measures
the beat reshapes.   The heart is pliable
until the world falls into a hard focus—
a deviation at the start of all things,
this life.   Upon the hem of your garment
we make abstract fabric. From stockpile rubble
this is how the long war begins: in a clutch,
a dream fevered   that lusts to shape the world.
Call this the red immense,   an abandoning,
a return to the blank page   and empty space
the halo point of any burning city.
There are language purists whose ears sever
contemplating the music   within a shape.

Surrender the Body

Try to forget and the body will remember for you.
It is not that we don't want to imagine. The penalty
for dream-making is having to watch the world unmoved
by you. There is only so much room, and men demand
so much space. The violence doesn't make you tough
like they said it would—just makes you quiet. Spend a life
shadowboxing against the unwritten wall, it can learn you this
real fast. Not having the words feels the same
as not having something to hit. Can't be a boy who doesn't
walk heavy. Got to find a way to make the weight. Ain't the one
that made the rules. Ain't gonna be the one
that can't bear it. Try to tell me I shouldn't want
these things—look at me and tell me I don't know
what happens when you ask for too much.

2

MY FATHER'S ENGLISH

This much is true with translations: words marry
to make a meaning. In Tagalog you say, hindi magtatagal,
it means, "not lasting"—this is the only way we say "soon,"
that thin slip of a place between "now" and "want,"
it cannot last, we do not wait, it will
will us to itself. It is why we say bahala na, "happen what may,"
though we mean this to say, "what leaves us
in God's hand." How we say God is a happening,
God is what happens.

In English, I wonder if God has become
my way of saying, "a thing just out of reach."
There is a place between languages
that can hardly carry the stubborn heart of patois,
that knows how a word can be home and foreign in the same
mangled pronunciation. There is a place between languages
where you learn to be ashamed
of your father's English.

I understand this language
more than I've ever wanted.
In poetry, I'm always asking
to make mine what can't be mine.

When I was a kid, my dad used to take me to the lake.
We'd sit on the benches and stare at the water for hours.
When we talked, it was always in English.
Sometimes he'd ask me how to pronounce the words correctly.
When he couldn't get one right, couldn't get that "z"
to sound like a "z,"
he'd say it again and again and again:
pi-cha, pi-cha, pi-cha.
It was so much effort; it's how I came to know
that anak means "child of mine"
and kain na means "let's eat."

This way of living, so far from living in.
The throw in my belly
is all the desire I was not supposed to have.
It's a way of wanting in this country,
a big stubborn heart
full of stomp and tremble.

STORY

As I can recall, every bit of telling
memory is a certain fiction. The truth
as best I can build it. The Philippines is hot: this is true.
Everyone looks at me and sees my father: this is also true.
When I leave the farm of the woman who helped raise him
(when the money was not enough), she, my grandfather's sister,
chases after me as I trod down the muddy path back to our car.
She cries and asks me not to leave her again. I feel
that this too is telling memory. The mist pulls into wide
when the body reminds itself: I memorize
her hands outstretched to God, sun stumbling across
the palm canopy. Her hands, the story. All her tears
folding into the rain.

What Is This Thing Called Want

A friend of mine once spent the year traveling the world on a boat because the feds raided one of her stash houses in Vegas; figured it was best to lay low for a while so she got to see Thailand and India, visited her motherland in China and hit up just about every party island in the Mediterranean. When she returned she called me with only the sparest of details: the bust, the boat, etc.— only really wanted to know about me. So I told her the truth: since the last time I saw her I'd moved back home because all my money ran out on me and now I see a therapist every two weeks. I told her I got fat because after all that time we spent fucked up I needed something, and the beer, it ain't like having a gin and tonic or a fuckin' Chardonnay, it stays with you, it's a slow burn, and sometimes I just need to hold on to something. I told her how I didn't really know how to be happy on my own anymore. Then she talked about how she enrolled back in school, went back to doing some stripping on the weekends, and how she was seeing somebody now; said he looked just like me but chubby, which meant now he did look like me.

The last time I'd seen her, we were at her apartment in Costa Mesa scrapping vials for just two lines we could snort before bed. There's a way in all this empty that makes more of your empty places, makes you remember you ain't been touched in a long time; so I asked her if I could sleep in her bed; said all I really wanted was for her to hold me. She laughed it off, like a woman who looks like her ain't had about dozens of other men and women try that same last ditch desperate move to fuck her and maybe that's what I was doing, but by that point I couldn't steady it all. Everything seemed like a good idea.

That day she called, I told her I couldn't resolve it. If everything was some kind of long-running lie we crafted because we were young, because it felt like believing in something, then I can't think about what that makes the last five years of my life. I told her I miss her like I miss the drugs. She asked if I was still using. I told her yes, sometimes.

A few days later my older brother and his wife had their first child. I slept through a morning full of voicemails and couldn't find a happy

louder than the hurt in my stomach. Puked twice before I even got
in the car and arrived at the hospital a wobbly husk counting and
recounting the number of his steps. When I got there she was cradled
in my brother's arms. He'd fallen asleep in his chair. I watched
the voiceless motion of her mouth reaching and pulling back and
reaching. What I did not know then is that this is how children
indicate their hunger, they search with their lips in hopes they will
eventually find it, some answer to the pull inside their bellies, a way
not to need so much. I took her and I actually sang to her.

Ma,

today you ask me to take you to the airport
so you can properly mourn for your older brother—
ten years have passed,
we swore we wouldn't wait
another ten years to come home,
but we always do. We always wait.
Life is flesh, Ma, and memory wounding.

Your older brother becomes a thing I try to make meaning of,
ghost with a man inside,
the shade we walk under.
It is the way people talk about losing memory,
the gaps, holes, a splitting of;
still, there is no fracture here
that empties clean.

Every memory of your home
is something a little kid would make up:
the airport littered with hay and loose dirt,
the uncle who kept a lion in his arboretum,
the night I couldn't sleep, saw a man with a horse hoof
cracking holes in the pavement.
My memory is not broken, it is torn across the grain;
there are mornings when I wake up
to the same sick that broke me
all those years ago in the sugar cane fields,
remembering the touch of the witch doctor's long fingernails
carving symbols into my skin, along my palms,
the bottoms of my feet.
They said afterwards I slept for two days.
All I remember:
a television playing in the living room,
the crackling of fish frying in oil.

What is this process of unmaking?
Who do we blame? The city grids, all this tract housing,
billboards and the strip malls?

Your magazines, or cable TV? My memory
more tabloid than tableau. Don't know who to blame.
Once a month we'd pray a rosary to the Virgin Mary statue
that passed around the block. We'd ignore the mirrors
in strangers' living rooms.

A few days after the sick ran through me
a devil of a rag dog chased me through
the streets of your city, had me cowering
on the hood of an abandoned jeepney.
I realized then there was really nowhere I could go
where I wouldn't have to run from neighbors' dogs.

I had feared so much in your country,
and on that plane ride home believed
there was only enough room for carry-ons
and God to fit in the overhead bin.

Sometimes, Ma, I forget your full name.
So much of you a foreign country
I left at an airline gate.

Today, the Role of Bruce Willis Will Be Played By My Dad

Sitting around the breakfast nook: my mother, carefully folding into herself, hands softening around the undone patchwork resting on her palms. My father's tongue a blunt device made heavier by the weight of his native dialect. He yelled, *Bakit!?* Why? Why can't you do these simple things? English words are unable to hold my father's passion. Maybe this is why my mother asked him, "Do you want to hit me?" He collapsed into a hard pause counterbalanced by a man's need to be right, to win. No, he told her, his jaw tightening to a pulse, walking away, her face reduced to dull pallor.

Later that day he took us to the movies and let me choose. I leveraged the morning's incident toward a movie with an R rating. Two hours into watching it: Bruce Willis gruffing his way through implausible feats of bullet-dodging and populist machismo, he finds his wife (assumed dead) in the middle of a snowy airfield and acceptable man tears well up as he holds her tightly in his arms. My father, sitting next to me, stumbles into a graceless attempt to wipe the tears that had begun. The laughter my mother was carefully stifling pistoned into a mild snort. *Umi iyak ka ba?* Are you crying, my mother asks. Resigned, he helplessly flails his arms at the screen—His wife, he said, He thought he lost his wife.

Magkampo

I.

The hornet's nest was a muddy heart pulsing
on the end of a long brush field, a trench lullaby
I still loved at ten, before I learned how to curl
a frail heart into a fist.
I was nothing like my cousins,
who rumbled in the waking world
and moved like loose rocks over surrendering hills.
They stood there arguing over who would be
the first to stir the nest,
so I grabbed the biggest rock I could find,
to prove I wasn't soft
and I could break beautiful things.

II.

I always thought there was something really weird
about a whole lot of Filipinos camping.
Not even three days in the deep woods
and we couldn't go one without somebody using the gas grill
to cook up a pot of rice.
In the Philippines, my father tells me,
the act of camping isn't recreational,
it's what you did when you didn't have a home.
And yet, every summer I was made to learn
how to find a place of quiet
where the sound of rustling leaves occurs on my body,
I learned how the stars should really look
when I draw them in my notebook,
and I walked on the world before everything
under my feet became pavement.

III.

We got pulled off the hike
by the bread crumb trail of heaving panting,
right into an orchestra of lush and mud
buried in the two-backed beast of a sloppily-built biker
and a woman he called "Mama"
sliding across each other like two slabs of warm butter.
My older brother sent me to move in closer
and see if there was anything we could steal.
Crouching behind a rotting tree
I couldn't help thinking how much more precious
this woman's face became against his palm,
how the centrifugal force of a kiss is
more real than what you see on TV.
When he pulled off her, walking away to complain about the bees,
she lay there, bare and open,
introducing me to a whole series of questions
I didn't even know how to ask.
I was as prepared for this as I was to find her
looking back at me:
shaking her head and smiling like my mother did
when she would tell me I was growing up too fast.

IV.

That night, my loss of innocence became
the running joke around the campfire.
My mother took a seat next to me;
I was sure I would be punished.
Instead, I drifted inside of her hard pause,
her hushed mother's prayer to the gods
of Please Don't let Me Fuck This Up.
She wiped the ashes off my face and asked
if I wasn't too big now to let my mommy hold me.
I shook my head, closed my eyes,
nuzzled my head against her.
The low crackling of fire
turned to a music box in my head.

V.

My father once bought me a cardboard clubhouse
I saw on the back of a cereal box. After he put it together
I fell backwards onto it and the whole thing collapsed.
It sounded just like the nest did when the rock left my hand,
like another thing I wouldn't be able to undo,
the sound of a thousand hornets suddenly woken from slumber.

No Shade Along the I-5

Here a tomato grew
inside of
my palm.

This is my work. I'm asking you to believe
that something here will grow. All faith is blind.
No one says a prayer with their eyes open,

but I have dug
for so long
to see a   such as this.

FOR JOSEPH, WHO DROWNED IN THE CREEK

It's always the boys   (we boys)
who mistake our heartthrobs for blunt instruments,
our arms bent, sinewy and strong enough to move mettle
like   I got the steel for this
like   I am not moveable   and men, real men, are foundations.

Why do we boys tempt the water when it wakes?
We boys, who know the armistice in its steady hum,
how we engage quiet's fickle fuse,
how we tuck it tight into the chamber of our palms.

Who prayed for the rain that day?
For the creek to build into a mean froth.
The white of its rushing, like a static pulse,
like bent teeth. The long descent into the ravine,
pushing through the brush, your dirty sneakers
rattling the creek at its streaming margins.
This much motion can make a lie of us,
these lives we made building ourselves into brick.

Ride

Every day during lunch break
Chuy Moreno would roll his '67 Chevy Impala
round the front of John F. Kennedy High School,
his chassis waving like a Palm Sunday frond.

He was sixteen, cheekbones raw with acne,
had a mean mug more metal
than his box grill. He was a carpenter
who was a carpenter's son. And learned enough

to know where to sign the contract, and where
commas and decimals belong in his paycheck.
Sometimes after cruising the roundabout
a few times, he would open his side door

and let a couple of the freshmen right in the backseat
while he hit the hydraulics. We'd sit, cross-armed
bending our mouths against our bottom lips, our mouths
that ached to say, Again, again, again, again…

History of the Ardenwood B-Boys

I'm from Fremont, California.
That shit was no South Bronx,

we never had Central Park,
Kool Herc plugged into the lamppost,
up-rock battles on the subway.

This is the history of the Ardenwood B-boys,
elementary school kids with brown skin
lugging around cardboard
meant by our parents to be used as Balikbayan boxes.

We knew three moves: groundwork, backspin, pose.
I been in love with Hip Hop since back in the day,

and, no, it wasn't the day I first heard Run DMC,
watched Beat Street, or threaded fat laces into my Adidas.

The day I fell in love with Hip Hop
I trace back to the playground of Ardenwood Elementary,
the day we stood up to the white kids
who kept us under knuckle and sneaker heel
with the same curses their parents had for ours.
What began as a high-noon standoff
between potty-mouthed children
burst into a chipped-wood pressure cooker,
it was only a matter of time before one of us popped.
Never thought it'd be the quiet kid, Neil,
who walked into the middle of the mayhem,
his provincial malnourished body
a steel girder through the tempest,
took every bit of it,
every bit of chipped wood,
every bit of burgundy spit flitted,
"Fuck you, white boy!"
"Fuck you, monkey!"

toothpick arms clenched
like a Moro warrior facing a Colt .45.

This was everything that defined Hip Hop for us,
who worshipped at the house of European gods,
who learned the words Washington, Lincoln
before we ever learned the words Bonifacio, Rizal.
We who were made to contort the nature of our tongue
to more easily pronounce the words
Assimilation.
Acculturation.

To tell you the truth, my crew sucked.
We looked like heroin addicts taking a tumbling class.
In time none of us followed the sprayed pathways of Krylon,
or lived between two turntables.
I made one rap school in high school—
it was called, "Bust a Freak Mode," so you know my shit was whack.

But you ask any one of us where Hip Hop is for us today,
and we'll tell you.

It's raising children.
It's fighting to pay the bills.
It's living split-lipped, bruised knuckles and an ear-to-ear grin.
And when another MC contemplates the death of Hip Hop
at his philosopher stone, I ain't ready to believe it.

At my base mettle,
I am still that kid hurling tanbark at America.
And yeah, sometimes I still dream of being a dope MC
but I tell stories like this one:

A while back I found my brother
curled up in a sleeping blanket on my parents' driveway.
When I asked him what he was thinking he said to me,
"I got these friends, B-boys from Hungary. Every night
they gotta sleep on the street to keep doing what they do,
I had to know if I loved the art as much as they do."
Embarrassment washes over his face as he says to me,

"You think I'm pretty stupid, huh?"
I take a seat, hold him tight, and tell him, "Not one bit."

3

SHAKING THE STEEL TREES

This is how the city welcomes us
into its arms of blank pages playing
minor chords on open elbows.

This city is a scorched vein. Its belly a rough-
hewn patchwork rumbling at the threaded margins

and I love you in this city, dear God I love you
in this city that makes romance
of the hiss bursting from a freshly cracked
bottle of your favorite beer.

This mashup city, this
composite scar harmony city, this
channeled flicker switch of a city
where every morning Love
is pulling an extra hour from the shelter of your spine.

The way you pull me across all this concrete
and bottle the world inside a city block.

How the fuck we end up here anyway?
One night inside the low tide of your slumber
and I wipe the entire week off my blackboard chest.

The weighted empty of my hands an encryption,
the distance between Manila and Chicago: 8,000 miles
slowly collapsing inside an Oakland bedroom.
How unlikely this should all be,
how less imposing these number become
across the wet crook of your neck.
A morning of my grandfather's lost memory of home,
the unrolling parchment of your grandmother's skin—
all this history in the open veil of your body,
this seed, this push, this silt,
how we been built by a blood procession of so many hands
pulling plough over poverty.

Love is a shifting probability;
but we been living in a shit economy wondering
What is Love supposed to conquer now?

But I love you in this city,
dear God I love you in this city
of boarded windows and missing unemployment checks,
this partitioned city,
this open-air crackhouse city,
this dream-severed city.

If I could still love you through this
skylight sweltering,
drumline pavement city of echoing footsteps,

if I could still love you when this city
is a trembling fistful of last chances
waving off the last round of eviction notices,

when this city is a groundswell pummeling,
when it is all split and marrow
and gutted promise,

this city, its canvassed arms mainlining,
riot gear and sulfur,
this city, its quake, its thundered hum,
its torch-lit streets

If I could still love you through this, this city
that speaks to its young in the burdened language of kindling,
this city of fight and forward movement,
of all the places a person can fall in love.
This city that falls so short of loving us
how we love it,

how we still keep tearing at the city's fist for its plum root,
how we still keep shaking the steel trees for fruit.

HAIKU FOR A FAILED RELATIONSHIP

Restless in the heat
your fists hammer my compact chest
no one blames the sun

THIRD MONTH IN AUSTIN

Is there something about the new city that wants
to tell you too much about yourself? Yesterday
was bargaining with the heat or the cicadas.

I used to sleep through freeway and rolling pavement.
Now it's too quiet so all the thinking gets too loud.
I don't know yet how one makes a home,
but I make great walls.

I believe
it's going to be better this way.
I have lost her,
she just hasn't said it. There's a place where I brick
so that people
will get tired
of throwing themselves against it.

At least tonight,
at 3am, I'm moving.

All the time people keep talking about the music here.
The other day I was saying, I still
haven't figured out where to find it.
Somebody walked to the front of the restaurant
and brought me the weekly paper. Everybody here
is so helpful. Didn't want to say, That wasn't what I meant.

GOD OF MISPLACEMENTS

What is the speed of living? Too much
wanting lining over the base. The difference between
needing to know, and knowing my place. The line
keeps moving over us. You can't see it. The line keeps
moving over us and every time we push, the push back
comes harder. We can say it shouldn't be there anyway.
All I got is to work with what is until it isn't anymore.

A Broken Crown of Sonnets
for the End of the World

I.

All I got is to work with what is until it isn't anymore
so I could give a fuck if the man on the radio is telling me
judgment is coming and how terrible it's going to be. Terrible
has already been here. We know terrible by the way it cuts

family lines and erases language until our words for God
and Love become unspeakable on our own tongues.
We know terrible by the way we turn from each other,
trying to avoid seeing ourselves because it reminds

us too much of ourselves. And so the old man says,
There is no place of Hell. Hell is a construction. What is meant
is the real reason people fear death. The idea of nothing after.
An empty space without movement. A place with nothing to name.

It's the least original idea, making heaven out of endings. Like rain
when it breaks, how that first crack of light is named, glorious.

II.

When it breaks; how that first crack of light is named, glorious
in all its destruction. It is still a destruction. There is a heft
to the clouds parting. Storms build. The tornadoes build until
they break. And what breaks we build again, while people
begin breaking inside themselves. It's easy to see the cycle,
not so easy to live inside it. It is not just the way of things,
it is what we endure. What gets done because it has to
be done. The cold can break you. The heat can break you.

And then there is all the hunger. The pull and all of its Must.
When they say Courage, or Bravery, or Heroic—how much
of it sounds like a point of access, something outside yourself.
I can't understand these like I understand Want. I know Want.

Its edges. How it pretends to be the hilt, then makes one of me.
If I could just
say   the difference between the whole and hole in me
                                        is the way.

III.

Say the difference between the whole and hole in me is the way
you move through it. So much talk about love and all
it makes. It makes a quiet, too. It can make you unhappy.
All the songs lied to you. You don't get back what you give,
you really don't get back what you give. But Love hungers
like any hunger. The fight in it, the growling push and monster
of it, when what I'm trying to say is… what I'm trying to
say is… all of language is dead-ended.

What is Love, then, but finding the right expression? The proper
        handle. Knowing how it loosens your knuckles. Being able to
        name the place: it is right here, the choke in my throat
when you tell me you can't keep living in my silence.
It is me climbing my way past all this comfortable alone.
Because I speak and the world is already full with endings.

IV.

And the world is already full with endings,
until all you're left with is all that persists.
That's what you do, isn't it? Every day
that you answer hunger, that's what you do.

A body is whole with it, what can be affixed
easily: the bang, the void, the empty space.
What we cannot name in good conscience.
Because we can't call it what it is, only what

we want it to be. Like when all of me wants
to curl into a fist, I believe its name is Defense.
Hitting somebody don't feel much like it, though.

I remember every one of 'em. Like knocking around
everything I ever hated about myself, until
everything that hit me back was everything I was meant.

V.

Everything that hit me back was everything I was meant
to own. Or so I've been told: God won't give me any more
than I can handle. Can barely work my way around language.
The headlines today make me feel, and I ain't got many places
to put feelings. You're going to make me say maybe. Maybe
things end. The bills are still past due and I'm looking
for a clock to punch. Maybe all this money is artifice—
I'll still be putting it down for another drink with friends.

This is the world for what you get in the gift baskets. Looking
at the linear, trying to map the points, playing who flinches first
with finite time. When you say there is an ending, it's because
you want someone else to say there is an ending—all these
I have names for, whether to call it Love or Displacement.
When I say my name out loud, I will wait to hear it back, that you
might remember me as a place in the world.

TROUBADOR

Oh Texas, I am losing myself.
When the mourning dove sings, I hear the wind
whistling down an empty alley in San Francisco.
And the gusts will hit the leaves and turn them
into a thousand wings that will bring me home.

So sing, bird, sing. I'm just a kid locked inside my headphones.
A grown man who sings too long in the shower. Some tattooed
knucklehead who listened to too much Teddy Pendergrass
and ain't giving a fuck if I sing that shit off-key.
For those who cannot lament or want properly,
the sad song will say it.
Someone find me, I want to go home.

One night I walked into a bar in Vallejo, California, down a strip
that turned ghost (when the city began to fall into bankruptcy)
into a bar lined with old men slouching into their beers.
What I remember most is how loudly Santana's "Samba Pa Ti"
resonated inside there. The song poured out of their glasses,
made their bodies into music boxes. I don't want to want like this.
It is an irrevocable condition. Oh, how we sing Home.

Oh, Texas. I am lacking permanence,
loosed in this gorgeous heat. I know it is gorgeous
by the ugly it makes me feel—the sweat got me.
I must be swatting the river on the back of my neck
and the sky keeps stealing the sun from my back pocket.
Only the bartenders smile at me. If I'm to be good with anything,
why not the bartenders. All I ever really want to do with people,
is hug them or hit them. Hate you or love you. All I want
to do is hug you or hit you.
It's what makes the most sense, when you
don't know what to do with your hands.

Growing up we were always told to look toward the future.
Nobody I knew ever really looked toward the future. If we had,
how many of us would say, "What terrible things you would leave us with."

When the radio starts counting the dead in Syria,
I am rifling through
a shoebox filled with pictures. I find one of her kissing me
in a photo booth. I took it with me the day I left.
And when the radio
repeats the dead,
I say, "Over there is a woman in love. A man in love."
They sing the dead and want does not lose itself to the casualty.
Want will drive the rock into armor
as easily as it will clasp hands to prayer.
It will carry into the smoke
of Damascus a hum and all its repetition.

My body is a projection of stone that remembers the mountain it
ran away from.

And tonight, I will run
right into another gorgeous night in Austin, Texas.
The whole body of me, a crooner, a soul singer,
some busker with a broken guitar
who sings of home
and all the wonderful things we wish to fill it with.

Continuum

… and what to do with all these damn poems,
an errant thread in the blood, the diving stitch.
How we hold the pieces together. The words
fall between the rolling seams of our skin.

I hold every unruly poem inside my skin.
Letters dressed in wick and rumble, the cantilever
set loose and flailing upon the narrowed lines,
my life told upon the slack and this poem,

this poem is a room, it is a room and it is me
inside this room and everything inside this room
has a mouth except for me. The walls are scratched
and burrowed, the air softer than my mother's fingers.

Inside, what I'm trying to say is, I remember this,
I remember windows, outstretched and pulsed.

B-Sides

MITCH HEDBERG

*"I'm tired of following my dreams man. I'm just going to ask them where
they're going and hook up with them later."*

What makes a comedy?
One part: an audience who recognizes it only by its most titillating factors
the other: a comedian who understands that this
is our most fully realized expression of grief

★

Mitch Hedberg died on March 29th,
three days short of the punch line;
or maybe not.

★

Suppose comedy bases itself inside of a flaw
a narrow crease tucked away inside of a constricted artery—
the great joke of your heart Mitch. It was made to fail.

★

In 1989, a long-haired fry cook living in his first apartment opens a
fridge with no food
he pulls an ice tray out of the freezer and calls it dinner—
tells his roommate, check it out, I'm an ice sculptor.
What did you sculpt? His roommate asks.
He pulls his hair away from his face, a curtain opening for his wide
mouthed grin.
He says to his roommate, I made cubes!

★

What makes something funny?
The part of me that knows how to answer this question
is a place completely devoid of humor.

★

This is a language that falls out of form: propped upon
consonants uncertain in their identity—

★

a consonant is defined by an obstruction of breath; a vowel is breath
the syllable is a sliver of life, but the word is duplicitous
the word is racked by double and half meanings;

★

is this why, when they told you the lady
was called Heroin
you swore she'd save your life.

★

Suppose that in the realm of deductive reasoning
comedy is what you would call the fallacy affirming the disjunct:

★

one speedball cocktail // a congenital heart,
still living // ain't dead yet
therefore, stick a needle in the vein that doesn't twitch.

★

Why grow old anyway? The world is filled with old men
who've talked about following their dreams;
who realized too late, that their dreams were sick of following them.

★

According to friends, to pull a "Mitch,"
one must sneak out the back door without saying goodbye to anyone.

FUCK A NOSTRADAMUS

The final chapter of this world
will not arrive at the ass end of a big bang.
It will congeal, it will rail upon its own significance.
It will arrive with an industrial size can of mustache wax
and DJ dance parties in gentrified neighborhoods.
It will think itself
pregnant with thought and fine cheese, preface
even the most trivial of its actions
as being done "Apocalypse–style."
It will quote itself often, in Facebook status updates:
I am the greatest disaster of this generation of this decade— The Apocalypse
Why won't you let me be great?— The Apocalypse
The end is nigh— The Apocalypse

The Apocalypse will dedicate 2 hours out of its day to write
long-winded blog posts about how everyone else
is *such a fuckin' douchebag*. It will mock your Spotify playlist.

It will be heralded by the roving band of shirt cockers
who speak only in the silent languages of *hey, look at my dick,*
can you see my dick? I'm just wearing a shirt with no pants
to accentuate the fact that my dick is hanging out, no reason
I like a cool breeze. Hey, is that my dick? It sure is.

We will learn that creativity had never died
it was busy trying to figure out how many different ways
we could achieve an orgasm.
There will be much pillow-fucking.
There will be much volume.

The Apocalypse will come
and it will become very upset
when you are not comfortable in its presence
because it makes them uncomfortable
and the Apocalypse does not like to be uncomfortable
especially when you stigmatize it with such trigger words as
extinction level event and organismist;

Then the Apocalypse will get mad at all the people,
say that they're the ones who are being organisimists against it,
and when the people say,
perhaps you don't understand the power dynamics at work here,
also, you're not an organism,
the Apocalypse will storm off, rambling about political correctness
and bootstraps; somehow it'll be the dead people's fault
for not being the civil ones in this conversation.

And there will be those who join the fray
there will be those who will claim to be above it
and there will be those who will write it off
as just one big corporate/freemason/lizard person conspiracy.

And we left will be the worst of all;
amongst the death and building fracture
all anyone will know how to talk about
is how this much tragedy really makes living difficult on them.
How we will still clamor for attention
from a diminishing audience.
And when we greet each other, it will not be
with a smile or a handshake, but a simple disclaimer
It's the end of the world and we're all probably gonna die soon,
wanna fuck?
It will be the bright spot of our humanity
our most precious act of giving
and the zombies, by this point
will simply lose their taste for us.

ABOUT THE AUTHOR

Jason Bayani grew up in the San Francisco Bay Area. He is a graduate of Saint Mary's MFA program in Creative Writing. He is also a Kundiman fellow, a veteran of the National Poetry Slam scene, and one of the founding members of the Filipino American Spoken Word troupe, Proletariat Bronze. Currently, he is living in Austin, Texas where he is an English Instructor.

ACKNOWLEDGMENTS

I'd like to send some love to the editors of *Fourteen Hills, Muzzle Magazine, Mascara Review, Tandem* and *Maganda Magazine* who printed some of the poems in this collection.

Thanks to those who helped me shape what this book would become over the years.

This is for my Mom and Dad. For Jake and Jonathan. For Jaeya, Alexis, and Logan.

For Mesej and Jaylee.

For Lauren.

IF YOU LIKE JASON BAYANI, JASON BAYANI LIKES...

The Undisputed Greatest Writer of All Time
Beau Sia

How to Seduce a White Boy in Ten Easy Steps
Laura Yes Yes

Time Bomb Snooze Alarm
Bucky Sinsister

Miles of Hallelujah
Rob Sturma

Glitter in the Blod
Mindy Nettifee

Write Bloody Publishing distributes and promotes great books of fiction, poetry and art every year. We are an independent press dedicated to quality literature and book design, with an office in Austin, TX.

Our employees are authors and artists so we call ourselves a family. Our design team comes from all over America: modern painters, photographers and rock album designers create book covers we're proud to be judged by.

We publish and promote 8-12 tour-savvy authors per year. We are grass-roots, D.I.Y., bootstrap believers. Pull up a good book and join the family. Support independent authors, artists and presses.

**Want to know more about Write Bloody books, authors and events?
Join our maling list at**

www.writebloody.com

WRITEBLOODY
QUALITY AMERICAN BOOKS

WRITE BLOODY BOOKS

1,000 Black Umbrellas — Daniel McGinn

38 Bar Blues — C.R. Avery

After the Witch Hunt — Megan Falley

Aim for the Head, Zombie Anthology — Robbie Q. Telfer, editor

American Buckeye — Shappy Seasholtz

Amulet — Jason Bayani

Animal Ballistics — Sarah Morgan

Any Psalm You Want — Khary Jackson

Birthday Girl with Possum — Brendan Constantine

The Bones Below — Sierra deMulder

Born in the Year of the Butterfly Knife — Derrick C. Brown

Bring Down the Chandeliers — Tara Hardy

Ceremony for the Choking Ghost — Karen Finneyfrock

City of Insomnia — Victor D. Infante

The Constant Velocity of Trains — Lea C. Deschenes

Courage: Daring Poems for Gutsy Girls — Karen Finneyfrock, Mindy Nettifee
& Rachel McKibbens, Editors

Dear Future Boyfriend — Cristin O'Keefe Aptowicz

Don't Smell the Floss — Matty Byloos

Drunks and Other Poems of Recovery — Jack McCarthy

The Elephant Engine High Dive Revival anthology

Everything is Everything — Cristin O'Keefe Aptowicz

The Feather Room — Anis Mojgani

Gentleman Practice — Buddy Wakefield

Glitter in the Blood: A Guide to Braver Writing — Mindy Nettifee

Good Grief — Stevie Smith

The Good Things About America — Derrick Brown and Kevin Staniec, Editors

Great Balls of Flowers — Steve Abee

Hot Teen Slut — Cristin O'Keefe Aptowicz

These Are The Breaks — Idris Goodwin

Time Bomb Snooze Alarm — Bucky Sinister

Uncontrolled Experiments in Freedom — Brian S. Ellis

The Undisputed Greatest Writer of All Time — Beau Sia

What Learning Leaves — Taylor Mali

What the Night Demands — Miles Walser

Who Farted Wrong? Illustrated Weight Loss for the Mind — Syd Butler

Workin Mime to Five — Dick Richards

Working Class Represent — Cristin O'Keefe Aptowicz

Write About An Empty Birdcage — Elaina Ellis

Yesterday Won't Goodbye — Brian S. Ellis

CPSIA information can be obtained at www.ICGtesting.com
Printed in the USA
LVOW071829220313

325680LV00002B/9/P